BORN FOR IT

90 DAYS & 90 WAYS

BORN

TO DISCOVER

FOR

YOUR GIFTS

IT

AND PURPOSE

CARSON CASE

ZONDERVAN

Born For It
Copyright © 2019 by Carson Case

Requests for information should be addressed to:
Zondervan, *3900 Sparks Dr. SE, Grand Rapids, Michigan 49546*

Library of Congress Cataloging-in-Publication Data

ISBN 978-0-310-7673-50

Interior design: Denise Froehlich

Printed in China

---

19 20 21 22 23   LSC   10 9 8 7 6 5 4 3 2 1

Foreword

Anyone who personally meets my man Carson Case knows he is the most passionate person for Jesus of our generation. The reason I stand so strongly for this book of devotions he has written is because I stand so strongly for who Carson is as a person. He's living his life exactly the way Jesus calls us all to live—abundantly and in the community of others. I don't care if you've been a Christian your whole life or hate Christianity, this book and what it has to say will make your life better. Maybe you picked this up by chance, but you're reading it now for a reason. We all desire a better life. A more fulfilled life. A life with passion and meaning. *Born For It* reminds us that no matter where you are in life—if you're a student trying to get through school, if you're working toward becoming a pastor or missionary, or if you are a stay-at-home mom, God wants so badly to use you to impact this world! What my good friend Carson has written is guaranteed to set a fire inside of you, encourage your soul, and remind you of God's ever-present promises.

Get pumped. Get excited. Get ready for a more fulfilling life. And let's jump in!

Cole LaBrant

Introduction

Have you ever questioned what you were made to do? Like who are you, what does it mean, and are you even gifted at anything in this life? I spent so many of my early years living without purpose. At seventeen, I was hit with an unexpected injury to my lower back, leading to immediate surgery. I lost any hopes of playing college basketball or football. At that point in my life, I spiraled into a search for hope and a new beginning. And I discovered who I was meant to be and what I was meant to do.

We weren't meant to do life alone. We weren't made for something ordinary. We were born for something. We must do away with the thinking that if we aren't raised or built up in a certain way, then God can't use us for something in this world.

There is an extraordinary call for you to use what God has given you and influence your world. You don't have to be the next preacher, but you can be the next **you**. No, you right now, have been born to do something. The *Born For It* mentality is one that believes in growing into what God has made you to do. Maybe you don't have it all figured out yet. That's okay. Maybe you're still searching for some answers. No problem.

Together we will seek what God has for you. We will start believing. We will take the steps needed to be the best we can be.

As you take baby steps and big steps on your journey, you will fail, make tough decisions, and gain/lose many people. At the end of the day, remember what God has spoken.

You have purpose.

You were made for a faith-filled life.

You need other people.

You have a story to tell.

My story didn't end when I got injured years ago—no, it had just begun. God saw a picture bigger than I could imagine. And now I'm walking in everything he had planned.

It's one thing to have direction and be good at something, but it's another thing when you live with hope bigger than yourself. When you grab hold of real hope, your best life will come into view. The life you were born for.

You are born for it.

Carson Case

"now is not the time"

Our generation believes everything should happen instantly and that life is like a microwave, that things should happen right when we want. But the whisper I've heard lately is "Not yet." The best things are built through many days and nights. You are being molded right now. You are being shaped. Your heart is taking leaps to new places. It takes time. Maybe you need to hear that you aren't ready. The job isn't yours yet. If you went to that college, you wouldn't be prepared for what you'd find. Even that dream you see, it won't flourish just yet.

God has put some of our wants on hold because he knows that if we had them right now, we would ruin them. We would ruin what we aren't ready for. I want to help you hold tightly to your dreams and to your process of getting there. Don't cheat what's on its way. Take a breath in your current situation and believe a couple of things . . .

YOU'LL BE READY IN DUE TIME.
YOU'RE GROWING, AND THAT'S A GOOD THING.
IT'S NOT OVER, IT'S JUST NOT NOW.

We also glory in our suffering, because we know that suffering produces perseverance.

ROMANS 5:3

DAILY DECLARATION

God, give me strength in my waiting so that I don't ruin what you've prepared for me.

don't hold back

_____

_____

_____

_____

_____

"making sense of your pain"

Yep, it happened. The hurt felt like nothing else, but you aren't there anymore. You are standing on new ground, in a new space—a new place. You aren't the you you used to be—and that's a good thing. I'm not writing this to tell you something new, I'm writing this to remind you: look how far you've come. Look at the peace you now have that you lacked long ago. Remember those tears you were crying six months ago? Remember that person who broke your heart and never came back? Remember the dream that failed over and over? Remember the pain your family went through? You need to know that you've made it this far and God isn't about to fail you now. He's standing next to you. Continue to step forward knowing that the pieces of the puzzle are falling into place. You're that much farther along, and a new season is on the rise.

THIS IS FOR THOSE WHO FEEL LIKE QUITTING NOW.
THIS IS FOR THOSE WHO NEED A FLARE IN THEIR FIRE.
THIS IS FOR THOSE WHO FEEL LIKE THEIR STRENGTH IS FAILING.

Consider it pure joy, my brothers and sisters, whenever you face trials of many kinds.

JAMES 1:2

DAILY DECLARATION

Give me peace in my pain and remind me that you're faithful.

don't hold back

_____

_____

_____

_____

_____

"see where this thing goes"

How about you give it a shot? I don't know what has been constantly aching on your mind, but you do. Right now, in this season, you have a decision to make. We all do. What is on your heart? Believe in it. Grab it. And don't let it go. This is that sign you've been praying for. This is the time. Maybe you've wondered. Maybe you've asked trusted people around you. Maybe you're at a point of no return. Say yes today. Not to the foolish things. Not to what used to be. Not to being an idiot and running toward what's not good for you. But yes to a leap of faith, yes to the thing that scares you but will pay off. It's been pressing on your heart for so long. God put it there, and it has purpose **right now**.

IT'S TIME TO DECIDE.
YOU HAVE YOUR YES.
RUN TOWARD THE WISE, NOT THE COMFY.

Not that we are competent in ourselves to claim anything for ourselves, but our competence comes from God.

2 CORINTHIANS 3:5

DAILY DECLARATION

Give me faith to trust that you are making a way, God, even when I don't fully understand it.

don't hold back

_____
_____
_____
_____
_____

"rip the roots"

I hope you haven't overlooked your foundation. That's where you may be missing it. Have you ever checked your roots? Your roots hold your strength. And right now you may be losing every ounce of strength, of faith or belief, that life could get better. Maybe you've let weeds grow in your soil. Maybe what's attacking your roots is something someone said or something you heard. Have you allowed someone's words to stick with you, to strangle you? Have you allowed some of the past to clog you up?

We need to rip out those weeds now. They aren't just killing your attitude, but they're killing your calling. Your roots are either poisoned or purposeful. Hold yourself responsible right now and do some digging. Don't give anything or anyone power over your foundation. Start ripping.

CLEAN UP YOUR SOIL.
SOME THINGS DON'T BELONG IN YOUR LIFE.
THIS IS YOUR RESPONSIBILITY.

First clean the inside of the cup and dish, and then the outside also will be clean.

MATTHEW 23:26

DAILY DECLARATION

It's time to remove things that are poison to my spirit and build a firm foundation.

don't hold back

_____

_____

_____

_____

_____

"leaving the land"

Goodbyes are no easy thing. Most of us hate to leave. We hate leaving people who were there for so long. We hate leaving places that had such a grip on our hearts. I believe there's some land you've been told to leave but you just can't release your grip. The things of old are pulling you back, holding you down, and keeping you from **more**. But with leaving the old comes new beginnings. What's keeping **you**? Can you put your finger on it? Is it someone who's meant so much but hurt you even more? Hurt will hold you captive. Or is the land you don't want to leave the land you've been used to for too long?

You have to be the one to cut the tie and move. Nobody is going to do it for you. The truth is, you weren't meant to stay any longer. It's time you get up and walk. The moment you leave will be the moment you sense the healing.

SAY GOODBYE.
IT'S TIME YOU TURN A NEW PAGE.
GOD HAS PREPARED SOMETHING NEW; NOW GO.

See, I am doing a new thing!
Now it springs up; do you not
perceive it? I am making a
way in the wilderness and
streams in the wasteland.

ISAIAH 43:19

DAILY DECLARATION

Something new is on the way for
me; it's time to step forward and
leave the old behind.

don't hold back

_____
_____
_____
_____
_____

"you're meant for this"

I t's time you get your swagger back. You left many things in your past, but you forgot to bring your confidence with you. Just because you've moved on doesn't mean you've lost your power. And remember, all your confidence doesn't come from your flesh; it's a God thing. Stand firm in who you are today. Stand firm in him. It's easy to transition into something new with a softer, quieter voice. But that isn't you. Yes, where you are now isn't where you've always been, so it's not as easy. But why let a new time in your life dictate your strength?

You have that confidence. And it's because God gives you that confidence. You excel at being the best you when you trust God. His power is yours when you let him lead. Yes, people will try to take that power or they'll be envious of it. But you know yourself—God made you this way. You were meant to lead with strength, walk with strength, and succeed in strength. Speak this over yourself: "I am confident, I am strong, and I am meant for a great life." Now it's time to live it. No more doubting yourself.

Don't let your confidence go missing.
Doubting yourself has no place in your mind.
Start opening your eyes and stop believing what isn't.

Have I not commanded you?
Be strong and courageous.
Do not be afraid; do not be
discouraged, for the Lord your
God will be with you wherever
you go.

JOSHUA 1:9

DAILY DECLARATION

I'm stronger than I think because God is making a way today.

don't hold back

_____
_____
_____
_____
_____

"don't be alarmed"

S top worrying so much about what they think. They don't even know you that well and you're breaking your back for their applause. Don't you know? Not everyone is going to approve of you. This should be no surprise. Since birth, you were called to be the best version of you. Each of us has been uniquely built. And our "builds" are surely different. Even though you are headed in the same Christ-focused direction as others, God may take you on a road that zigzags every which way. Don't turn back now. You are being chiseled by his perfect hand.

When others see you succeeding at what they aren't good at, they may get angry. When you're making moves, people may become envious. When your authenticity shines through your life, people may want it for their own. Don't you see? You can't stop your train just because others fail to understand you. I wouldn't be alarmed. They may never get you—and that's okay. God approves of you. All you need is his stamp. Hold on to who you are and what you've set out to accomplish. Stay confident in your journey, because that's what matters. Keep the faith.

YOUR WORRIES AREN'T AS BIG AS YOU BELIEVE.
TAKE A MOMENT TO REFRESH YOUR FOCUS.
YOUR PURPOSE IS YOUR PURPOSE, NO ONE ELSE'S.

Am I now trying to win the approval of human beings, or of God? Or am I trying to please people? If I were still trying to please people, I would not be a servant of Christ.

GALATIANS 1:10

DAILY DECLARATION

I'm confident because I'm not living my life to please the rest.

don't hold back

_____

_____

_____

_____

_____

"fill up your cup"

I know you're more tired than you put off. You're the "mom" or the "dad" of the group. It seems that no matter what, you're always available to those who are hurting. Sure, it's a good thing. But, hey, what about you? You aren't taking care of yourself; you're too busy worrying about the next person. You think it's honorable. And it might be. But now you're out of gas and you're hurting yourself. Stop. Find some time and space to fill up **your** cup. This doesn't mean you have to leave the ones you love; it just means you need to retreat to those who can pour into you for a change. Stop pouring it all out.

So today is **your** day. Make it about you and go find what you need. You know why? Because if you keep running on empty and refusing God's strength, you'll be no good to anyone.

Don't mistake fatigue for failure.
Your life starts with your health.
Taking care of yourself cannot be last any longer.

> Then God blessed the seventh day and made it holy, because on it he rested from all the work of creating that he had done.
>
> **GENESIS 2:3**

DAILY DECLARATION

God, you've given me something to take care of. It's time I tend to myself well.

don't hold back

_____

_____

_____

_____

_____

"this isn't the worst of it"

I t isn't easy now and it may not be easy for awhile. But you signed up for this. You chose to trust God. Maybe your family and friends aren't understanding your decisions, but you've trusted in a hope much bigger than yourself. Didn't you know what you were doing? Don't let the storms, the criticisms, or the hardships rob you of your strength and determination. They are all teaching you to grow even in your discomfort.

Now is the time to find your inner strength. Find the ones who want to fight with you. Believe right now that God is on your side. Even though you are weak, your strength isn't completely gone. And what's worse is if you choose to do it alone. This struggle wasn't meant to be lonely. You are going to experience a second wind, and what now seems like an obstacle will be a catalyst for the "even harder" things to come. I want you to see this as training. This isn't the worst of it—and it's okay. You're getting stronger. It's time you believe that.

YOU ARE JUST IN TRAINING, GETTING STRONGER.
YOU AREN'T ALONE RIGHT NOW.
YOU KNEW THIS WOULDN'T BE EASY; DON'T START BELIEVING DIFFERENTLY NOW.

I consider that our present sufferings are not worth comparing with the glory that will be revealed in us.

ROMANS 8:18

DAILY DECLARATION

God, I'm stronger because of these struggles and, with you, I will only keep getting better.

don't hold back

_____

_____

_____

_____

_____

"you're planting the right seeds"

Isn't it so easy to get frustrated with the mundane? The small things? The moments no one sees? The tears and the hard work? I know it is true because I've lived it too, but the parts will come together over time and the blur will turn into clarity. You may not see it yet, but you're making a way. Not just for yourself but for people around you. See, that's why you have to stay in the process. Because even the smallest of moves creates a path. Those conversations are getting you somewhere. Those heartbreaks are molding you. Clarity is on the way. Do you believe it?

Look, what you're doing right now is going to pay off. I don't care what doubt has creeped in. Or what lie you've been told. There's power in what you're doing. It all plays a part in what's to come. You can't forget these days. How great it's going to be when these seeds grow into what God always wanted them to be. You'll look back, and you'll thank God. You just don't know it, can't see it, yet.

YOUR SEEDS ARE SINKING INTO THE RIGHT PLACES.
SMALL DOESN'T MEAN INEFFECTIVE.
YOU'LL LOOK BACK AND SEE THE POWER OF THESE MOMENTS.

Jesus told them another parable: "The kingdom of heaven is like a man who sowed good seed in his field."

MATTHEW 13:24

DAILY DECLARATION

God, you're doing something with even the smallest things in my life. I believe it.

don't hold back

_____

_____

_____

_____

_____

"people need people"

Yep, you need them. You may not like them right now. You may be upset. You may need a moment in your room, your own space. But isolation is your key to desolation. You can't do this journey by yourself. Have you not looked around at those who have done so much for you? You've spent all this time criticizing and swimming in negativity—and you've only lost sight of those people you need. You've walked away from their wisdom. In moments of frustration, it seems like your way is a lonely highway and no one understands, but you'll regret this way.

You know what you need to do. Go back. Go back to the ones who care for you. Deep down, you know who you need. I trust that you'll take a breath and see the truth of your situation. You can't let anger take hold of your future. The people around you matter, so wait, breathe, and see beyond your feelings.

YOU CAN'T DO THIS ALONE.
ANGER BURNS BRIDGES.
ISOLATION LEADS TO DESOLATION.

Share with the Lord's people who are in need. Practice hospitality.

ROMANS 12:13

DAILY DECLARATION

Remind me that I can't do this long road of life by myself.

don't hold back

_____

_____

_____

_____

_____

"your excuses aren't helping"

God made you for things you can't even dream of, but you're sitting around? You're wasting your time? Get up. I know the family you come from doesn't have much money. I know school isn't your cup of tea. I know Dad isn't around much, if at all. I know that heartbreak ripped your life apart. I know, we know, it hurts—and we all have a story. But God didn't intend for your story to stop you there.

You were born for something; no one is going to do it for you. The truth is it's time to flee your excuses. If you don't, you'll lose sight of who you could be. Come on. There was a time when you set those goals, you made promises, and you had the fire. You've talked too long about "what you would do if . . ." Let's get your fire back. It has to start in your heart because what comes from your lips comes from there. Excuses have no place in your space. Here's your opportunity. Let's go.

No more wasted steps.
No more excuses.
No more maybes.

Whatever you do, work at it with all your heart, as working for the Lord, not for human masters.

COLOSSIANS 3:23

DAILY DECLARATION

Lord, give me a fire again for what you created me to be passionate about.

don't hold back

_____

_____

_____

_____

_____

"you are addicted"

It's gonna hurt talking about this. It feels like you're sitting in a prison. And I'm not talking at you, I'm talking with you. Many of us have been there, in a "cell," wishing we could walk away from what's binding us. You're hooked on it. It's been robbing the joy out of your life. You're clocking in hours daily, allowing **that** substance or **that** thing mastery of your heart. I don't want to see you like this anymore. Let today be your last straw. Take a baby step out of imprisonment. Maybe you need to cut someone off or leave a situation altogether. But stop your life from being tied to something that gives you no free reign to have an abundant life.

This isn't about a magic fix or an easy road—it's about a hope. Not an empty hope but **real hope**. Freedom is a life we choose. That freedom is in one name, and I know that name to be Jesus. Today is your day.

YOU HAVE THE HELP YOU NEED TO EMBRACE THE HOPE.
THAT PLACE ISN'T YOUR PRISON ANY LONGER.
FREEDOM IS A LIFE YOU CHOOSE.

Therefore do not let sin reign in your mortal body so that you obey its evil desires.

ROMANS 6:12

DAILY DECLARATION

I'm declaring a new hope in my life today. Freedom is for me.

don't hold back

_____

_____

_____

_____

_____

"painting the picture"

We all have our moments, and I believe yours is now. It doesn't matter where you're from, what you're studying, or what you aren't good at—you need to paint a picture for yourself. Every young person needs a vision. Stop looking at where your friends are, or you'll miss where you are. Sure, Mom and Dad may not understand, but they aren't supposed to, at least not now. Did you know that, from day one, God had something orchestrated for your life? Not just "because," but because you have someone who believes in you. You aren't alone, and you aren't without the tools. That means confidence starts now. That means you have to kill comparison and embrace what's right in front of you. You're in the right city. You're in the right school. You've got a few friends. The tools are yours. Now what are you going to do?

I'm believing with you. I'm expectant for your future. God didn't make a mistake with what's inside you. So start fighting for what you've always wanted to do—because it's yours. Don't allow anything to steal that which was tailor-made for your abilities. Paint the picture.

YOU'RE RIGHT WHERE YOU NEED TO BE.
YOUR VISION IS IMPORTANT.
COMPROMISE CAN CRIPPLE YOU.

Then the LORD replied: "Write down the revelation and make it plain on tablets so that a herald may run with it."

HABAKKUK 2:2

DAILY DECLARATION

God, help me act upon the vision I have. You are up to something in me.

don't hold back

_____

_____

_____

_____

_____

"are you going to live with power?"

My past attempted to highjack my power. But I won't let it. Have you ever thought about that before? Your past will do whatever it can to shame you into thinking you're too weak to move forward. Maybe it's because someone hurt you. Maybe those people never believed in your potential. You know there's a future for you, but it's been nearly impossible to put away the heartache of the past.

Here's the thing though: You've lived like this for too long. You've wasted time. You've wallowed in your situation so much that you think you're meant to stay in that "hole." Not any longer. I'm declaring power over the now and the future. God wants to use you. Not for who you used to be or what you've dealt with, but for who you are becoming. The past has no hold on you anymore. The breakthrough is today. Live in it. Clear eyes, full hearts, can't lose.

YOUR PAST HAS NO POWER ANYMORE.
HEALING IS HERE.
YOU'RE STRONGER THAN YOU CAN IMAGINE.

So do not throw away your confidence; it will be richly rewarded.

HEBREWS 10:35

DAILY DECLARATION

I'm breaking through my old hurts and experiencing better days. My heart is full!

don't hold back

_____
_____
_____
_____
_____

"well, you've never been here before"

The beauty of unfamiliar territory. Don't you just love it? I'm kidding. It's terrifying, and we all know that. Once the world as we know it begins to change, it's easy to allow fear, anxiety, and doubt to creep in. We want to plan our next steps. We want a road we can see. But if we could learn to embrace what we **don't know**, we could open doors of miracles. See, when we venture to new places and new things, it means growth is ahead of us.

You may not recognize where you're stepping or even the people who are coming along with you, but you'll see. It's called trust. You have to believe that new places don't determine you're "dead meat." You were born for more than you think. Your life may take you down routes you didn't plan, but this is bigger than you. Trust. This new place you're in is the way to a life beyond your dreams—even if you don't fully believe it in this moment.

A NEW PLACE GROWS A NEW YOU.
DON'T LET FEAR LEAD YOUR NEXT SEASON.
YOU WERE BORN TO TRUST.

He put a new song in my mouth, a hymn of praise to our God. Many will see and fear the Lord and put their trust in him.

PSALM 40:3

DAILY DECLARATION

This new place is sure to grow me into who God is calling me to be.

don't hold back

_____

_____

_____

_____

_____

"what about your parents?"

We are constantly fighting for the approval of people around us. It's a battle for our generation to be who we are called to be. In the midst of your journey, sometimes your parents may seem like they want to hold you back from who you are. This isn't a word, a permission, to pull you away from them, hate them, or disrespect them—but here's a need to know: what God made you for isn't tied to your parents. Maybe you believe me or maybe you don't, but I'm here to say that your call is about you. You're not being selfish. You're being real. Your gift starts with you.

So, no, they may not understand where you're headed. They don't have to understand your new job or your latest passion. They don't need all the answers to your post-high school choices. Stop crowding your brain with the thoughts that you have to be who they want you to be. It's time to grow up. Let God be the one to help them understand when the time is right. Trust that he knows your parents better than you do. You use your passions, abilities, and talents to change the world. Follow what God's best is for **you**.

WHAT THEY THINK DOESN'T DETERMINE YOUR DESTINY.
YOU DON'T NEED TO BE UNDERSTOOD.
BE REAL AND TRUST God'S LEADING FOR ONCE.

Trust in the LORD with all your heart and lean not on your own understanding; in all your ways submit to him, and he will make your paths straight.

PROVERBS 3:5-6

DAILY DECLARATION

God, show me that you have a way for me even if my parents don't understand where I'm going.

don't hold back

_____

_____

_____

_____

_____

"the power of someone else"

What's all this talk about finding someone? Why are you even looking right now? You're praying for what you aren't even ready for. You don't need a relationship right now. It could weigh you down and keep you from becoming what you need to be. Yes, I said it. It's time to work on you. You've neglected it for too long. Stop looking online. Stop searching your DMs. Put the phone down. Focus. The more time you put into searching, the less power you're gaining in your own journey.

Right now, it's time to take charge of your life. You don't need any extra weight. Own your life. Today marks a new road where you release the need for someone else. Stop letting that hold you back from your best.

YOU KNOW WHAT YOU NEED.
DON'T FALL FOR DISTRACTION.
TAKE CHARGE OF WHAT'S IMPORTANT IN YOUR OWN WALK.

Therefore do not worry about tomorrow, for tomorrow will worry about itself. Each day has enough trouble of its own.

MATTHEW 6:34

DAILY DECLARATION

I will not be distracted any longer; I've got to take charge of what's mine.

don't hold back

_____

_____

_____

_____

_____

"stop playing catch up"

Being you is the best thing about you. Let me rephrase that: You don't need to be anyone else. Your timeline is yours. God-given and God-planned. Why are you rushing around like you need to level up with the rest? Have you begun to believe the lie that if you aren't up to par with the next person, you've failed? No! Your time is on the way. It may take four days, four weeks, or four years, but that's not what matters. What matters is that you stay true to who you are.

You have a road to run. Don't believe for a second that you've fallen behind. You haven't. Your path is just different from those around you. As long as you stay in the lane you've been given, it will be blessed. Follow your road. You've got this.

YOU MUST BELIEVE IN YOUR TIMELINE, IT IS GOD-GIVEN.
YOU HAVE A ROAD TO RUN.
YOU AREN'T BEHIND; YOUR PATH IS JUST DIFFERENT.

I will instruct you and teach you in the way you should go; I will counsel you with my loving eye on you.

PSALM 32:8

DAILY DECLARATION

I don't need to rush, God has a road tailor-made for my life.

don't hold back

_____

_____

_____

_____

_____

"are you settling?"

You may be in a situation right now where those around you, the dreams you're dreaming, and the things you're believing are "compromised." You aren't living in a lie, but you aren't being fully honest with yourself either. You didn't begin your life seeking mediocrity. None of us did. We all long to be the best we can be. There's something for all of us, but settling can rob us of even that.

I want you to look around you. Is it valuable? Is it up to your standards? How much work have you really put in? Check your current relationship; is it the best? What about your group of friends; how do they treat you? And your personal health—are you just going through the motions? You can't make a move unless you see where you've settled. Seek to find where you've compromised. Make a change if necessary. You don't want the potential of your life falling further and further away from all it is meant to be.

Now to him who is able to do immeasurably more than all we ask or imagine, according to his power that is at work within us.

EPHESIANS 3:20

DAILY DECLARATION

God, I will not settle for less than your very best in my life.

don't hold back

_____

_____

_____

_____

_____

"get out of your cell . . ."

It feels like the bars are getting cold, right? You've been holding onto them for days, weeks, and months now, shaking them and shaking them, asking for help to break free. It's not that you aren't able; it's that you need help. It's time to open yourself up. You can only do so much from in there. But if you shout it, then someone will hear you. Start a conversation with someone you trust. There is someone who is here to listen to your story and give you freedom. The longer you allow that darkness to swallow you, the harder it'll be to speak. Please don't be embarrassed by what you've been through. Everyone has their demons. Others have spent long nights in a cell but they are free now. They can help. I don't want you in there any longer. Someone is ready to listen and listen today. You have a voice; speak up. Love is not lost. Freedom is not too far away.

YOU'VE BEEN HERE TOO LONG.
TRUST SOMEONE ELSE.
YOUR STORY IS NOT OVER.

Now the Lord is the Spirit, and where the Spirit of the Lord is, there is freedom.

2 CORINTHIANS 3:17

DAILY DECLARATION

I'm not too far gone, and the battle has not been lost.

don't hold back

_____

_____

_____

_____

_____

"remember this"

Remember right now. Feel the discomfort. Feel the pain. Feel the tension. It's part of your story. These moments are molding you and making you. It may be the complete opposite of what you wished or prayed for, but this is when you will find out more about yourself than you bargained for. You will see your hurt. You will see your reactions. You will see the friends who are true. You will even see God work in ways you've not yet seen.

So mark these moments in your mind and learn to focus even when you want to give up. These moments will test and stretch you more than you thought possible when you started. Let it toughen up your skin and teach you. Then you'll never forget how you got through it.

FEEL WHAT YOU FEEL.
REMEMBER EVEN THE WORST OF IT.
MARK THESE MOMENTS.

A woman giving birth to a child has pain because her time has come; but when her baby is born she forgets the anguish because of her joy that a child is born into the world.

JOHN 16:21

DAILY DECLARATION

God, these moments are molding me for my future. I won't forget the lessons in this.

don't hold back

_____

_____

_____

_____

_____

"when you blame your pain . . ."

Yep, you've been hurting for a while now, and maybe you don't know anyone else who has been in this situation. It feels like the whole world is caving in. The pain is what started it, but you let it continue. You lost someone. You got injured. Your family isn't like it used to be. You've been through the worst imaginable, and you've mourned. And someone else could have done something to change it or prevent it.

Your pain is no longer by itself. You've attached blame to it. And you got stuck there. Your blame is locking up your progress. Now it's a crutch and an excuse to wallow rather than set out and do what you need to do. You don't think there's a way to move on? I guess this is it then. No! Put an end to that thought. I want to see you get out of bed. Stop the blame game. Release those you think are responsible. You don't know their story; you don't know their pain. You can only take responsibility for yourself. It's called ownership. Look at what's in front of you and act. You can't hold yourself prisoner any longer.

BLAME CAN'T BE A CRUTCH ANYMORE.
BEGIN AGAIN.
IT'S TIME TO MAKE SOME PROGRESS.

Jesus looked at them and said, "With man this is impossible, but with God all things are possible."

MATTHEW 19:26

DAILY DECLARATION

God, I feel like I've gone through the worst. I won't let my pain hold me down. I won't blame anyone else for being stuck.

don't hold back

_____
_____
_____
_____
_____

"the courageous one . . ."

Maybe this day seemed like nothing but a far-off worry that could never happen, but it's here now. Your mom has breast cancer. Or the college you hoped for didn't accept you. Or the friends you thought you'd have for life flaked on you. Maybe you've experienced a sudden death, and you're in shock. Out of all the scenarios, the one thing that remains the same is this: You must find courage. You must find courage because the circumstance isn't going to change. It will still be there when you wake up. And, nope, it probably won't make sense tomorrow or the next day either. But there's a calling on your life to take courage and keep going.

It's okay to feel the hurt. Let the tears fall, and yell at the sky hoping for another answer. In these moments, life will push you like never before to find something within yourself to cope. Let it be courage. This pain will not always feel this way. And even though you can't change what happened, you can change the way you face it.

FIND COURAGE.
THE CIRCUMSTANCES ARE FINAL.
THERE'S POWER IN HOW YOU APPROACH IT.

Be on your guard; stand firm in the faith; be courageous; be strong.

1 CORINTHIANS 16:13

DAILY DECLARATION

I won't let fear or pain keep me from courage. With God, I am courageous.

don't hold back

_____

_____

_____

_____

_____

"poisoning the well"

Your core is running every part of your life. I'm talking about your soul. See, you have a well inside of you. Everything starts from the inside out. Things are flowing, from relationships to dreams to conversations, and much more. What happens if you allow garbage in from the outside? It will contaminate the greatest part of you. You can't afford that. Maybe you're already at that point: too much garbage. Some of your conversations have been going from north to south quickly, and you can't even keep up. Some people are influencing you sideways, slipping in their subtle opinions and maybe not-so-subtle lifestyle.

If you don't start taking time to filter out the negativity, it'll poison you. Just make sure you really remove what's needed. Then start filling up—with the healthy things, the ones that will endure, the ones that will build a better future. Better now than never. It'll pay off.

YOU MUST TAKE CARE OF YOUR WELL.
YOU ARE TAKING TOO MANY RISKS WITH YOUR SOUL.
DON'T GIVE NEGATIVITY ANY ROOM.

Above all else, guard your heart, for everything you do flows from it.

PROVERBS 4:23

DAILY DECLARATION

God, help me take better care of my soul so that I don't let poison capture who I am.

don't hold back

_____
_____
_____
_____
_____

"what pain does"

It's hoping to blindside you and keep you down. Yep, that's the pain that you are feeling now. I know you've tried wishing it away, you've tried praying for better, and you've done all you can to make it go away—but it just won't. Pain is not your friend, but it may be useful. Have you realized that you have an opportunity to use it? Yes, pain can have a place in your story.

Pain either paralyzes you or propels you. Let me encourage you to let whatever pain is in your life now to be a propeller. You know you can't hurt like this for the rest of your life. You know that a new day is coming, and that joy is still yours for the taking. So don't let pain have its way in you. Seize a new perspective. Yes, your pain may have a purpose, but the purpose is not to control the way you live. You have an opportunity now to move forward. Get up and walk.

PAIN EITHER PARALYZES YOU OR PROPELS YOU.
PAIN HAS A PURPOSE.
DON'T LET PAIN DICTATE THE REST OF YOUR JOURNEY.

Blessed is the one who perseveres under trial because, having stood the test, that person will receive the crown of life that the Lord has promised to those who love him.

JAMES 1:12

DAILY DECLARATION

I will not let these things paralyze me or rob me of the opportunities that are to come.

don't hold back

_____

_____

_____

_____

_____

"creating space for rest"

Yes, you feel worn out right now because you aren't taking time to chill. You've been running around doing anything and everything and overlooking what's needed for your heart. What do you think will happen? You give all your energy to outside things. The media, better yet, other people's lives, has become your addiction. You haven't stopped going out in weeks. Give the keyboard a break. It's okay to enjoy some things, but when they have enslaved you, you've got a problem. You aren't missing as much as you think. If you keep going like this much longer, you'll lose you.

It's time to pause. Take a break. Cancel that meeting. Stay home from that party or text that person "no." You are wearing yourself down, and for what? Learn to retreat. Sit with God. Play with your own thoughts. Kick your shoes off and know that your life will be better if you take a rest. If you never rest, you never have time to hear what's next. And if you don't hear what's next, you can't be ready. Because rest equals readiness. Rest, ready, then go.

STOP GIVING AWAY YOUR ENERGY SO EASILY.
IT'S TIME FOR A BREAK.
YOUR REST WILL READY YOU.

For anyone who enters God's rest also rests from their works, just as God did from his.

HEBREWS 4:10

DAILY DECLARATION

God, I'm saying yes to a break. I'll be blessed with rest.

don't hold back

_____
_____
_____
_____
_____

"the one for me"

I s it an obsession yet or does it feel like one? You know what I'm talking about. How come they have a person to love on and you don't? Where is your person? Can't God just give you what you want? Why do you have to wait? Where is he? Where is she? It may sound simple, but there's much more to this. It's more about becoming who you're meant to be first. God may have a person out there for you to choose, yes, but a rushed and unorthodox pursuit is not your best answer. Stop creating your own timetable. What do you need to work on? Take your time.

As much as you want someone to date, it's easy to lose your own joy wishing for it. Here's what I mean: you can have joy despite not having a "special someone." Yes, your life has the potential to be incredible without anyone else. You weren't born to exist for someone else; you were born to have a purposeful life—with or without someone. The one for you can't replace that joy. So find that first.

STOP OBSESSING; START INVESTING.
STOP RUSHING GOD'S WORK.
FIND YOURSELF BEFORE YOU GO LOOKING.

Hold on to instruction, do not let it go; guard it well, for it is your life.

PROVERBS 4:13

DAILY DECLARATION

I will not be obsessed with finding someone else to fill my God-sized void any longer. It's time to take care of myself.

don't hold back

_____

_____

_____

_____

_____

"tired of this lifestyle"

L ife isn't what you thought, and the fun has started to slip away. It has become tiring, and deep down, you're hoping for more. Every young adult will hit this spot one day or another when you've spent too much time trying to build a life to impress people you don't really know and who don't care much about you anyway. You've hung around them, cut corners, and hoped it would all make sense, but here's the answer: there's more to your story. You never needed to build your life on sand or on nights you can't remember with people who couldn't care less. There's a life you're meant for. It's time to ditch the worn-out lifestyle of empty pursuit.

I want to tell you that God is for you, and your story matters. He has a purpose for what you've been through, but your life needs a change. Will you take the second chance he's giving you?

YOU HAVE A STORY THAT MATTERS.
THIS IS A SECOND CHANCE.
GOD'S ARMS ARE OPEN.

"Go, stand in the temple courts," he said, "and tell the people all about this new life."

ACTS 5:20

DAILY DECLARATION

There's a better life for me, not built on sand, but built on purpose.

don't hold back

"it's not this serious"

We feel a pressure to make things happen and stay busy. If we aren't busy enough, does the world think we are even worth it? I'm telling you now, you won't ever gain the approval you're longing for in that screen, with those people, in that role, or for that accomplishment. Those things only offer surface-level value. Learn to step back from this "rush." Remove this box the world wants to put you in. The expectations to "be productive" aren't really this high. Going and going to make sure everything fits perfectly is unrealistic. Nothing will ever fit perfectly. There will be hiccups. Some things won't work out. And if you allow the perfectionist mentality to rule your heart, you'll be disappointed daily. There's a price for losing yourself to striving for perfection. The world may be asking you to "do" a lot, but God isn't.

Take a step back. Look at where you are. Remove the unrealistic expectation. Sit and be thankful for the progress you've made, no matter how far you **think** you have to go. Kill the rush because it's not worth it.

You're living with unrealistic expectations.
Take a step back.
Busy "success" is not worth your soul.

> What good will it be for someone to gain the whole world, yet forfeit their soul? Or what can anyone give in exchange for their soul?
>
> **MATTHEW 16:26**

DAILY DECLARATION

God, I am not bound by any expectations. The progress I've made is enough. It's okay to stop.

don't hold back

_____

_____

_____

_____

_____

"you need saving"

I t's okay to not be okay. It's okay to admit when you've fallen. It's okay to be broken and beat up. We all are. I want you to know that you have a story, a purpose, and a place in this world. There's a safe haven for you. There's a home to run to. Maybe you never had a place to go before. But now you do. It's going to take honesty and vulnerability, though. You know what you need, but you keep running. Is it pride? Is it shame? Is it fear? The truth is that you need a Savior—not a religion or some list of rules but a person of hope whose name is Jesus. So enough of all the hard talk and loose ends. Come clean. Take this step and grab hold of this hope.

YOU KNOW WHAT YOU NEED TO DO.
EVERYONE NEEDS SAVING.
THIS HOPE IS FOR YOU.

For God so loved the world that he gave his one and only Son, that whoever believes in him shall not perish but have eternal life.

JOHN 3:16

DAILY DECLARATION

Help me to be honest about where I am and trust what I may not understand.

don't hold back

_____

_____

_____

_____

_____

"it was good, but move on"

That season was incredible. It seemed like blessings were everywhere and nothing could go wrong. The people in your life made sense. The days were good. And then things started changing. Why did it have to change? It's time to move on. A new season is on the rise. Some people have to leave. Others are ushered out by a power higher than we can control. Keeping your mind stuck in the pleasures of the past will cloud your view of what's new and coming. It was good then and can be good again, but it may take some time.

I know being in a new season isn't always fun. But I hope you know that the uneasiness of transition won't always be there. The new things want to welcome you. This season has a blessing that you can't see yet. Good is on the way. So don't let your mind be paralyzed by the past. Move on.

APPRECIATE WHAT WAS.
REALIZE THAT CHANGE IS ON THE WAY.
FIX YOUR EYES ON THE NEW SEASON.

Joshua told the people, "Consecrate yourselves, for tomorrow the LORD will do amazing things among you."

JOSHUA 3:5

DAILY DECLARATION

I will not stay stuck in what used to be when it's time to move on.

don't hold back

_____

_____

_____

_____

_____

"just a phone"

We don't like to be honest about certain things—and our phones are one of them. Ever notice how much time you've given to that little device? It's sucking up your potential to take on your real life. It's not that it's the worst thing in the world, but a distraction? Big time. It's been distracting you nonstop this whole season. Someone tries to have a conversation? You choose the phone. When you know you need to be somewhere? You've let the phone choose you. I don't know whether to call it addiction or slavery; it could be either or both.

We have to be real. That little piece of metal and plastic has you by the throat. It's getting out of hand and tripping up your progress. Do the hard thing and put it aside for a few hours. Limit your time throughout the week or do something as simple as turning it off and putting it away during food and conversation. No longer let this thing distract you from what's real.

YOU ARE MISSING YOUR REAL LIFE.
YOU ARE LIMITING WHAT COULD BE.
REMOVE THE DISTRACTIONS.

Listen to advice and accept discipline, and at the end you will be counted among the wise.

PROVERBS 19:20

DAILY DECLARATION

I declare a life of freedom from my phone and distractions that draw me away from what's real.

don't hold back

_____

_____

_____

_____

_____

" you're ignoring your potential "

The couch is getting old, and the complacency isn't fooling anyone anymore. You had the grades. You had the skills. People saw your potential. You've always been a winner. But you got comfortable. There's more in your tank. Have you realized that yet? I won't allow you to play pretend anymore. Get up. Responsibility is in your lap. People are counting on you and asking more of you. Isn't it embarrassing that they see it too? Sure, you wish life were simpler, but you can't waste this time. You weren't born to sit around. Everything you have is meant to be used.

Life will pass you by more quickly than you think, and then what? All that you had? All those dreams? The people on your side? Wake up; wake up! You're ignoring what you know. Open the box of your potential. You'll see what you're made of. We are waiting.

POTENTIAL IS INSIDE YOU.
OTHERS ARE COUNTING ON YOU.
WAKE UP AND MAKE IT COUNT.

Guard the good deposit that was entrusted to you—guard it with the help of the Holy Spirit who lives in us.

2 TIMOTHY 1:14

DAILY DECLARATION

Lord, there's more in me than I've shown. It's time to use what I was born with.

don't hold back

_____

_____

_____

_____

_____

"let's do an image check"

We often try so hard to create an image of ourselves for the world to see. It's put together through a filter. No blemishes. No cracks. Yet the filter is easy to see through. Why would we compromise who we are to please the world? All for painting a pretty picture that's fake? The problem is that we don't truly love who we were created to be. Because if we loved ourselves that much we wouldn't spend half our time trying to re-create our image for others, hoping they'll press "like." We've missed the mark.

We need more "heart work" and less "ego work." Building this false image isn't helping our inner happiness, joy, hope, or view of ourselves. It's hurting us, and we often don't even realize it. So can we put a stop to this? It's time to be real. It's time to celebrate who we truly are. It's time to love ourselves.

THE FILTER IS FAKE.
NO COMPROMISING WHO YOU REALLY ARE.
GOD LOVES YOU; NOW, YOU LOVE YOU.

"Therefore everyone who hears these words of mine and puts them into practice is like a wise man who built his house on the rock."

MATTHEW 7:24

DAILY DECLARATION

God, I will not compromise who I am any longer. My life belongs to you.

don't hold back

_____

_____

_____

_____

_____

"how's your soul?"

Anyone ever ask about your real life? How are you **actually** doing? I know it's rare; I wish it wasn't. But it's a good thought. Are you **really** taking care of yourself? Deep down in your soul is where you need to deal with the pains and the hurts, the fear of the future, and your hopes for tomorrow. Culture says keep the outside pretty and the rest will take care of itself. But that's not what we are going to believe here. Nope, we will stand on truth. The truth is that your life starts deep within.

Search inside yourself. Maybe you need to throw some things in the garbage. Maybe you have some pain that needs to be spoken. In these moments of soul-searching and soul declarations, we can find healing. Ask yourself, "How is it **really** going?" Because it's probably not going the way you tell everyone it is. Deal honestly with yourself. If you want to grow, to be better, you've got to work out what's in you before people can begin to see things through you.

Ask yourself how you are really doing.
It's time for real talk.
Everything works from the inside out.

> Why, my soul, are you downcast? Why so disturbed within me? Put your hope in God, for I will yet praise him, my Savior and my God.
>
> **PSALM 42:11**

DAILY DECLARATION

I will have a healthy soul over a pretty life. That's what I will build my life on.

don't hold back

_____

_____

_____

_____

_____

"loving your crew"

Everyone has a crew. They hit the lowest of lows with you. They show you comfort even when the world isn't comforting. Have you found yours yet? Are they on your team? Are they at your school? Are they at your workplace? The thing about your crew is that it doesn't have to be big. You only need a few to fight for you when the going gets tough.

A real crew talks less and does more. When your home doesn't feel like a safe haven, it's your crew who will create one for you. When your parents split up, it's your crew who will give love when it seems no one else will. A crew creates community, a place of refuge when you feel like there isn't one. So to the one reading this who has your crew, love them big time. Show your appreciation and thank God for them. Support them. And if you haven't found yours? There are people out there who want to run this race called life with you. No one is meant to run it alone. Go find them.

YOUR CREW GIVES COMFORT.
A CREW TALKS LESS AND DOES MORE.
YOUR CREW NEEDS YOU.

Carry each other's burdens, and in this way you will fulfill the law of Christ.

GALATIANS 6:2

DAILY DECLARATION

I will run a race with people who push me in love and action. I will not try this life alone.

don't hold back

_____

_____

_____

_____

_____

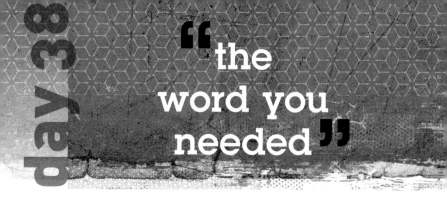

"the word you needed"

Have you heard something recently that tickled your ears, something you thought made sense for a friend but not for yourself? So often we think others need a "word" or a correction more than we do. That word might just be for you. The word you're deflecting toward someone else could be a divine voice saying, "**You** need this!" You need the help even though you don't think you do. You need a change. You need a healing. I'm just telling you that if you don't listen and work on yourself, all you're doing is finger pointing.

When we think less of others than ourselves, we demand more from them. When we think more of them and less of ourselves, then we demand more of ourselves. Yep, chew on that one for a while. God speaks over our lives—even through other people—so that we can grow from it. So get off your high horse. Listen up. This word is for you.

THINK MORE OF THEM AND LESS OF YOU.
YOU NEED THIS.
GOD HAS A WORD FOR YOU.

I pray that the eyes of your heart may be enlightened in order that you may know the hope to which he has called you, the riches of his glorious inheritance in his holy people.

EPHESIANS 1:18

DAILY DECLARATION

I've got some growing to do, so I'm here to listen to what God has for me.

don't hold back

_____

_____

_____

_____

_____

"here for your appointment"

Ever find yourself in a place where you expected good to happen? You sense that once you show up, something there is meant for you. It means you've been appointed. It means the moments ahead aren't happening randomly. They're preparing you for what's to come. See, we all have our appointment—moments specifically created for our talents and abilities. But we know that showing up isn't enough. We've gotta engage. We have to play our part. We have to learn to be present.

Let God know that you are here for your appointment. But also know that not everyone is in your favor. Those around you may not agree where he is taking you. They may not even believe in your talents. So naysayers, doubters, and old friends will have to be put on the back burner. What actions do you need to take now to ensure your focus? Keep showing up with strength, and let the world know you are here to get yours. It's appointment time.

YOU HAVE AN APPOINTMENT.
IT'S OKAY IF NOT EVERYONE IS IN YOUR FAVOR.
YOUR TALENTS ARE MEANT TO BE USED HERE.

Then the word of the LORD came to Jonah a second time: "Go to the great city of Nineveh and proclaim to it the message I give you."

JONAH 3:1–2

DAILY DECLARATION

I'm here because God meant for me to show up. Help me play my part.

don't hold back

_____

_____

_____

_____

_____

"why is it this way?"

Something new is here. I know the [insert hurt] may not make sense. You're praying for healing yet the heartache is beaming down on you. You don't feel ready for something new. You may be questioning your place and asking why in these moments. Asking why is part of the journey. We can be skeptics some days. It's okay to question. But constant questioning of every new situation and every new change is an easy way to make yourself bitter. Bitterness plants hate. You don't need those roots growing deep into your skin.

You're in a new place because there is something here for you. Yes, there's a reason it is the way it is—even if you don't know it. You must believe that. Ask your questions, but then move the why aside so you can embrace what's new.

QUESTIONS ARE OKAY; JUST MAKE A MOVE TOO.
BITTERNESS WILL DESTROY YOU.
BELIEVE THERE'S SOMETHING FOR YOU IN THIS NEW PLACE.

Now faith is confidence in what we hope for and assurance about what we do not see.

HEBREWS 11:1

DAILY DECLARATION

Lord, give me faith that there is a reason for right now.

don't hold back

_____

_____

_____

_____

_____

"the burden of boldness"

Being bold for truth carries weight. But bold steps aren't for everyone. Chances are people are looking for someone like you to step out and do something. It's boldness that builds up your strength. It's bold steps that shine a beam on important issues. It's boldness that paves the way for change and action.

When you're working for change, you'll face a wall of opposition. It may seem like an extra burden, but it's true that stepping out has its consequences. Don't expect everyone to understand what you are doing or even why you are doing it. Although you will gain opposition, many eyes will be on you because of the courage you've chosen to show. Carry that responsibility with confidence, knowing that boldness will pay off.

BEING BOLD WILL GET YOU INTO "TROUBLE."
BOLDNESS BUILDS STRENGTH.
KEEP CHOOSING COURAGE.

On their release, Peter and John went back to their own people and reported all that the chief priests and the elders had said to them. When they heard this, they raised their voices together in prayer to God.

ACTS 4:23–24

DAILY DECLARATION:

God, fill me up with boldness to take on whatever you have for me.

don't hold back

_____

_____

_____

_____

_____

"you've committed"

You knew this wouldn't be easy. You knew that hard work and commitment awaited you when you said yes. That relationship is going to take work. That goal is going to require persistence. Being on that team is going to mean endurance. You can't just sign up and then quit when the training gets tough.

You are going to face obstacles the rest of your life, so you must know that hard work is one of many. When you commit, you aren't just saying yes to the present. You are saying yes to the future. You are in the building process, and a lot more commitment is yet to come. Your commitment is bigger than you. People are counting on you. You aren't going to let them down, are you? In truth, your opportunities exist because of the hard work and commitment of others who've gone before you. Give them honor. Your commitment leans on the shoulders of others. So stay in the game, and you'll be blessed because you continued even when it was hard.

THIS WON'T BE EASY.
YOU CAN'T QUIT NOW.
DON'T LET THE DISCOMFORT ROB YOU OF THE BEST.

"And may your hearts be fully committed to the LORD our God, to live by his decrees and obey his commands, as at this time."

1 KINGS 8:61

DAILY DECLARATION

I will stay committed no matter the cost; I know my hard work is part of a bigger picture.

don't hold back

_____
_____
_____
_____
_____

"getting through the mud"

Did you expect smooth sailing? I hope not. We live in a crazy world. But here's a need-to-know: All the obstacles from the past and the ones you're facing right now, matter. They have been preparing you for now. Remember when your family was going through that cancer? It was breaking you down and then building you back up. Remember when your heart was hurt so badly you never thought you would heal? That hurt allows your heart to fill with compassion. I know, at the moment, life may feel like you are dragging through the mud, but God has been strengthening you for months now. This "mud" is part of your journey.

Count all the moments you thought you were finished. You didn't fall; you kept going. Where you are now isn't the end either. As you keep fighting, obstacles will still come. You will get through this not by knowing all the answers but by hoping in the strength God has given you along the way. Today, speak confidence over what's dragging you down. You will experience healing. You will grow from this. It isn't the end of your road. You aren't done.

THIS ISN'T WHAT YOU THOUGHT, AND THAT'S OKAY.
YOU AREN'T FINISHED.
YOU WILL GROW STRONGER.

We are hard pressed on every side, but not crushed; perplexed, but not in despair.

2 CORINTHIANS 4:8

DAILY DECLARATION

Lord, this isn't the end of the road; better days are ahead.

don't hold back

_____

_____

_____

_____

_____

"i need that lighting"

L ighting? The right angles? The perfect posting time? Do you realize how caught up you've been with these trivial things? Give it a break. You aren't living for your social status. And the truth is most people watching your social life don't care about you in the way you think. It's time to live the way you were meant to—with purpose—instead of dressing up every part so people will approve of you. It's less about the perfect posting time and more about being **on time** for those who love you for you.

Take this to heart: what you win people **with** is what you will win people **to**. If it's the small posts of your Instagram story, then yes, that's all people will ever expect from you. It's time you search a little deeper and think a little more. Taking care of your heart and soul, that's what matters. Invest in your real life. Life will be okay even if you forget to swipe the next story or post the next photo. You are **much more** than that.

YOU DON'T HAVE TO DRESS UP YOUR LIFE ANY LONGER.
TAKE CARE OF WHAT MATTERS.
INVEST IN WHAT'S REAL.

I have seen all the things that are done under the sun; all of them are meaningless, a chasing after the wind.

ECCLESIASTES 1:14

DAILY DECLARATION

My life is much more than my social media, and I will live to the fullest.

don't hold back

_____

_____

_____

_____

_____

"some will always hate"

Are you living to please the critics or are you walking exactly as who you are meant to be? Being authentic doesn't hold the promise of being liked. It's time you understand that. The world wants you to be someone you're not and like the things that you probably don't. You cannot sacrifice who you really are for the world because there will continue to be naysayers. There will always be people who judge your every move, not because they dislike you but because they are envious of who you are becoming. Don't forget that people are for you even when some are against you.

Here's the truth: you were created with a purpose that has nothing to do with what others think of you. Your uniqueness will continue to shine as long as you let it. So protect who you really are and scratch away any thought that says you will compromise for the crowd. You won't. You must continue living out your story because you are your best you. Let that be your confidence when you feel less "liked."

NO ONE EVER PROMISED YOU WOULD BE LIKED.
CONTINUE TO LIVE YOUR STORY.
NAYSAYERS WILL ALWAYS EXIST.

"If the world hates you, keep in mind that it hated me first. If you belonged to the world, it would love you as its own. As it is, you do not belong to the world, but I have chosen you out of the world. That is why the world hates you."

JOHN 15:18–19

DAILY DECLARATION

I will live with confidence that depends not on those around me, but on what is inside of me.

don't hold back

_____
_____
_____
_____
_____

"late-night memory lane"

Here you go again, overthinking every little thing in your life. You keep going back to what should have been or what you hoped for. We all know what that's like. It puts us in a mental prison and stops us from going forward. These nights are all too familiar for most of us. Put on an old, sad song or grab the car keys and go for a 12 a.m. drive to lament what happened? We've all been there.

The memories and thoughts from the past are clouding your vision. Your focus can either be your tool or your downfall. You have to find a healthy place to focus on. And you can't hold yourself hostage. Get out of your bed. Get out of that mindset. Maybe it's time for that prayer you've been scared to pray. That's where you can find the power you need to overcome your past and calm your mind. Don't allow what happened back then to ruin your future.

STOP OVERTHINKING.
START PRAYING.
FIND A HEALTHY FOCUS.

Finally, brothers and sisters, whatever is true, whatever is noble, whatever is right, whatever is pure, whatever is lovely, whatever is admirable—if anything is excellent or praiseworthy— think about such things.

PHILIPPIANS 4:8

DAILY DECLARATION

God, I will no longer let my thoughts run wild. I must find focus today on what is best for my life.

don't hold back

_____

_____

_____

_____

_____

"starting small"

Why can't it be an overnight process? Making a dream happen? Breaking an addiction? Getting better grades? Becoming your best version? The truth comes in time, not with a quick fix. There is something valuable about taking your time, addressing the right things, and focusing a little more . . . being intentional. It's not on your timetable. Baby steps are still steps. Tiny seeds still grow into full plants. Wouldn't you rather plant with precision instead of planting to fail?

There's always a starting point. Even in the smallness, there is power. You have to be wise right now so that certain things can run their course. You don't need to have all the answers right away. Take the steps as they come. Those seeds you are planting now will affect your future. They will affect your friends. They will affect your family. So believe in the small starts even if you'd prefer a much bigger and brighter situation. Down the road, you'll look back at the baby steps and say, "Wow, I never knew what that meant until now."

THERE IS NO QUICK FIX.
STARTING SMALL WON'T KILL YOU.
KEEP UP WITH WISDOM.

> "[The kingdom of God] is like
> a mustard seed, which is the
> smallest of all seeds on earth.
> Yet when planted, it grows
> and becomes the largest of all
> garden plants, with such big
> branches that the birds can
> perch in its shade."
>
> **MARK 4:31–32**

DAILY DECLARATION

I may not see it now, but God is
doing something here. I'm going
to believe even in the smallest of
steps.

don't hold back

_____

_____

_____

_____

_____

"i need some fruit"

You've gotten your rest and taken a little time off, but you are too talented to sit any longer. You've got the right people around you. You know it's time to plant, so let's get moving. Go ahead, get off your couch and turn off the Netflix binge. God hasn't brought you this far just to sit and watch. You were meant to produce.

You may not feel popular or full or even relevant to the world. But have faith—your life has a lot to offer. It just may take a little hard work and a bit more patience. That thing you've been dreaming of for months now, that prayer you've been praying— those things have a place in your life today. If you don't sow, then what is there to water? And what is there to grow? It's the season to start sowing. Down the road, you'll see the fruit.

SHAKE OFF THE DUST.
GET MOVING.
PLANT THE RIGHT SEEDS TODAY.

I planted the seed, Apollos watered it, but God has been making it grow.

1 CORINTHIANS 3:6

DAILY DECLARATION

I won't get stale or complacent. God, help me sow what's needed.

don't hold back

_____

_____

_____

_____

_____

"too many voices"

This isn't just a free-for-all. You can't go any longer getting tossed left and right by the voices in your head. You are giving the reins of your life to too many people. That's what's driving you nuts. Everyone seems to have a say. You need some direction in your life.

If you want to be successful and confident, you can't let everyone in. It's not just you who is in charge in your life, but in order to be led, you have to step away from all these other voices. Give the steering wheel to the one power who can truly guide your life, the one voice who is truly in charge. As you start loosening your grip a little, the other voices will fade and you'll be better off. God wants to take you somewhere. Trust his voice.

STOP GIVING EVERYONE A SAY.
TRUST THE BIGGER VOICE.
YOU NEED DIRECTION.

Commit to the LORD whatever you do, and he will establish your plans.

PROVERBS 16:3

DAILY DECLARATION

I will listen to the one voice that matters more than any other.

don't hold back

_____

_____

_____

_____

_____

"you're in over your head"

I'm just going to come out and say it—you are over-doing it, and it's hurting you. I know you have so much to do. The work is piling up. The studying is much more than you thought. And you have your own dreams. Your social life is taking a hit because you don't know who to turn to half the time. Not to mention the hit your soul is taking as stress keeps adding up. You keep trying to multi-task and find shortcuts. Who are you overdoing it for anyway?

It's time to hand it over. What I mean is your ego. It's time to take a look at everything on your plate. What is worth it? What isn't? What can wait, and what needs attention right now? The answers are probably not what you think, especially when you take your ego out of the picture.

GIVE UP YOUR EGO.
HAND OVER WHAT IS TOO HEAVY.
IT DOESN'T ALL REST ON YOU.

You will keep in perfect peace those whose minds are steadfast, because they trust in you.

ISAIAH 26:3

DAILY DECLARATION

God, remind me that I don't have to carry all of this.

don't hold back

_____
_____
_____
_____
_____

"you talk too much . . ."

Our words will only take us so far. People are watching you more than they are listening. They are looking at what you post. They are checking your Snapchats. You can't fake it till you make it. That won't work any longer. Either you're all talk or you're all walk. So get to work. The world is already full of too many big mouths. It's time to stop talking and start walking. Sorry if that's harsh, but you've talked nonstop about that dream. Now take the steps.

If you're going to commit to some of the things you're tweeting and posting about, we need to see it. When you start doing the work and people see the fruit, you'll get the respect. So be a doer. Make your words count on a daily basis. Make them real.

WALK IT OUT.
PEOPE ARE WATCHING WHETHER YOU LIKE IT OR NOT.
ACTION GETS YOU RESPECT.

But someone will say, "You have faith; I have deeds." Show me your faith without deeds, and I will show you my faith by my deeds.

JAMES 2:18

DAILY DECLARATION

I'm going to be about this action. I'm going to walk the walk.

don't hold back

_____

_____

_____

_____

_____

"overlooked but worthy"

Someone lied to you. Someone hurt you. Someone may have not wanted you or neglected you. Please turn off those comments. The ones speaking hate over your life. If you keep letting these people and their words into your life, you will feel unworthy. Don't you know your worth? What's true is that your worth does not depend on them. Your worth does not depend on what you are going through or experiencing either. Your worth is a God thing. I know others may not see it or call it out in you, but God made you on purpose. He is your worth. He has spoken it over you. Therefore, you don't need it from anyone else's mouth.

You are worthy and built for a life with meaning, one that will make sense down the road. God won't change his mind. He means what he says. You belong to him. Know your worth.

TURN OFF THE LIES.
KNOW YOUR WORTH.
STOP TRUSTING WHAT ISN'T TRUE.

For you created my inmost being; you knit me together in my mother's womb.

PSALM 139:13

DAILY DECLARATION

I'm not who they say I am; I belong to God.

don't hold back

_____

_____

_____

_____

_____

"not as good as theirs"

Holy cow! You've been scrolling for three hours now. How many moments of your life have you missed because you're caught up in someone else's? Sorry if that stings a little bit, but really, aren't you seeing it? The pictures you see are just pictures. We all know that those pictures have been carefully selected and edited over and over. You've let their life get in the way of yours. Their life may be a good one, but there's no way I'm about to let that take away from the good in yours.

This is about revealing the truth. This is bigger than social media. This is about destiny. Stop obsessing about "their" life, letting it disrupt yours like this. You know I'm right. Put down the phone. Turn off what you need to turn off and get to work on your life. Your life has so much more to it. Open your eyes to the blessings you're missing and the plan that was designed just for you.

STOP COMPARING YOURSELF.
PUT DOWN THE PHONE.
OBSESSION ISN'T YOUR CALLING.

Each one should test their own actions. Then they can take pride in themselves alone, without comparing themselves to someone else.

GALATIANS 6:4

DAILY DECLARATION

I'm done letting obsession with another's life steal from my own. I won't allow it.

don't hold back

_____

_____

_____

_____

_____

" in the palace "

It's never a bad thing to feel good about where you are. That's the blessing about being in the "palace." You worked so hard to get there. Your trust is strong. Your confidence is at an all-time high. You feel as if a lot has fallen into place. But you have to be careful now because you won't be in this spot forever. Life is full of seasons, and we never know what may come next.

When you're on a life high like this, you can become vulnerable to the ways of the world. So ready your spirit. While you're here, while life is good, dig a little deeper. Have your fun, and be thankful for where you are, but please do not get too comfy here. Prepare your heart, know your purpose, and remember where you came from. Another new season will come.

ENJOY LIFE WHEN IT'S GOOD.
APPRECIATE WHERE YOU ARE.
TIMES WILL CHANGE.

As for God, his way is perfect:
The Lord's word is flawless; he
shields all who take refuge
in him.

PSALM 18:30

DAILY DECLARATION

**Lord, I'm in a good place and
incredibly thankful. I know it
won't always feel this way, so
help me appreciate it.**

don't hold back

_____

_____

_____

_____

_____

"in the pit"

Y ou don't have much money. You're in the midst of making huge decisions. And God is pressing you to grow like never before. You'd love to laugh it off and say that life is "all good," but it's not. You feel as if you're in a dark place. It's hard to give God control of all things, even the simplest things like your money and how situations are coming together. You may be freaking out and feeling pressure. Yes, this is an uncomfortable place. You may even feel like you'll have to scratch and claw just to keep going.

There's a **word** over your life: hope. You won't be in the pit forever. What you're lacking now (money, time, clarity, love . . .) is not what you will lack in the latter days. God will guide you out. There is hope; there is a lifeline.

YOU'LL GET THERE.
THE DARKNESS WON'T LAST.
LET HOPE PREVAIL.

Being confident of this, that he who began a good work in you will carry it on to completion until the day of Christ Jesus.

PHILIPPIANS 1:6

DAILY DECLARATION

God, this pit won't be my end because you are still at work.

don't hold back

_____

_____

_____

_____

_____

"is there balance?"

You have a million things on your mind and your list. You've got a job or are trying to find one. You have a dream you want to see fulfilled. And maybe you can catch up on that video series, find a date, and work out during the week. Can there be balance in any of it? Figure out what is most important. It's time you get your priorities in order. Because if you don't, you'll lose sight of what's needed. And please, stop rushing. Balance is hard to find when you're moving too fast. You say you want to take better care of yourself, but you can't seem to get away from the weeknights out.

As you are learning to set your priorities and find balance, first find poise. Poise is going to start with a deep breath. Poise helps you pause and gain composure. Then you can make decisions one by one. Slowing down isn't the worst thing. As you step back a bit, you'll find the gaps in your life and what real success is. Celebrate some wins rather than always mourning the defeats. Therein is your way to balance. One task at a time. You got this.

YOU DON'T HAVE TO PLAY CATCH UP.
LEARN TO FIND A PAUSING POINT.
THE RUSH WILL HOLD YOU BACK.

I can do all this through him
who gives me strength.

PHILIPPIANS 4:13

DAILY DECLARATION

I'm not in a rush today, and I will find balance in due time.

don't hold back

_____

_____

_____

_____

_____

" success in staying... "

Please learn to stay. I know it's hard because others have walked out on you, and you may not have many friends. But something special in your spirit is meant to be there for people. It's part of who you are. Staying is the harder choice, and it doesn't always make it fair or comfortable, but you can help more situations and more people than you think. Faithfulness comes in knowing when to stay. And when people fall and reach for someone, that someone will be you.

You are special because you see value in others that most would ignore or forget. You can call out the best in people. You pick them up when they fall and sit by them until they are ready to walk again. People will remember your loyalty. The world needs you. Keep going with that kind of compassion.

YOU CARRY SOMETHING SPECIAL.
FIND A WAY TO BE THERE.
COMPASSION IS A CALLING.

Greater love has no one than this: to lay down one's life for one's friends.

JOHN 15:13

DAILY DECLARATION

I'm going to be a stayer; I'm going to be a friend whom others need.

don't hold back

_____

_____

_____

_____

_____

"you may not like it here"

Ever feel like you're in the wrong place? It's like walking into a party and feeling the stares of everyone because you don't belong there. As hard as this is to say, sometimes that's life—you feel as if you don't belong at all. Where you are isn't where you think you should be and you're constantly struggling with where you fit in the grand scheme of things. I know the feeling. So many of us are wishing for a new route or a new plan. Isn't there a different way to make this all work?

You're getting way ahead of yourself. Maybe where you are isn't the position you hoped for and maybe you think "this isn't me," but the truth is you have to give it a chance. This is the reality of your now. Your circumstances are what you have. What will you do with them? It's time to flush away the resistance and dig up some confidence. There is something here for you.

JUST BE WHERE YOU ARE.
GIVE IT A CHANCE.
SEE WHAT'S HERE FOR YOU.

When he saw the wind, he was afraid and, beginning to sink, cried out, "Lord, save me!"

MATTHEW 14:30

DAILY DECLARATION

I may not like it here, but there is something here for me. I will find it.

don't hold back

_____

_____

_____

_____

_____

"right on time"

Whoa! It's hard to believe this happened! For months now it seemed like nothing was adding up or working out in your favor. I'm with ya. I know that kind of experience. But isn't the timing interesting? You were doubting, like we all do at times. How did this happen? You scored the date even in your doubt. You made the team even when you thought you played just average. The money came right at the moment you thought it missed you. I'm not saying prosperity will always be the answer—I'd be lying if I did. But something has to be said about believing. You should try it.

Faith will unlock possibilities you never imagined. Believe that the time will be right. That even what you haven't tried to believe before could happen now. For such a time as this. Life won't always add up. But there's something funny about timing. Someone is working for your good at just the right time.

YOU MADE IT.
THE TIME IS RIGHT.
THINGS ARE WORKING FOR GOOD AND GLORY.

There is a time for everything,
and a season for every activity
under the heavens.

ECCLESIASTES 3:1

DAILY DECLARATION

**I know I've doubted in the past,
but my time is now and it's
good.**

don't hold back

_____

_____

_____

_____

_____

"how far you've come"

You've served your time, and you've made it count. It's obvious the fun you've had, but it's coming to an end. It's smart to look back. Look at how far you've come and what you've accomplished in a short amount of time. You met this person. You conquered that fear. You were able to start working toward that dream. All in all, you've become a better you.

I'm so glad that seasons come and go because it allows us to see our growth. So, yes, celebrate this time. And celebrate the past. Then set your heart toward a new journey. I don't want you to miss what's on the way. You may not know what that is yet or where to go, but new doors are going to open. You'll see. All you need now is to stay ready.

LOOK HOW FAR YOU'VE COME.
YOU'VE BECOME A BETTER YOU.
NEW DOORS WILL OPEN.

The eyes of all look to you, and you give them their food at the proper time.

PSALM 145:15

DAILY DECLARATION

God, I enjoyed what I've been through but I'm declaring something new.

don't hold back

_____

_____

_____

_____

_____

"a place you never wanted to be"

Sometimes we find ourselves in situations that have become so "normal" to us we fail to see the effect they truly have on our hearts. Maybe it used to be just for fun. Get together with some friends, throw a party and experiment. But now, it's serious. The late-night choices haven't just led you to this place, they now control your life. Maybe you never thought you'd be here, but it's real now. It's not fun anymore; it's a need. This is no longer a game, especially for those who love you the most.

Take a step back today. Be honest about where you are. What has become so normal that you stopped noticing the cost to your soul? How much longer will you allow these things to control you? I want to reassure you that your situation is not too far gone. There's more for you. Let's believe together that today you can leave this toxic place. A healthier future is ahead.

BE HONEST ABOUT WHERE YOU ARE.
IT'S GOTTEN OUT OF CONTROL.
LEAVE THIS TOXIC PLACE BEHIND.

I lift up my eyes to the mountains—where does my help come from? My help comes from the LORD, the Maker of heaven and earth.

PSALM 121:1–2

DAILY DECLARATION

No matter what I've done in the past, I can leave it behind for a new life.

don't hold back

_____

_____

_____

_____

_____

"living for the night?"

Do you rush through your week just to get to the weekend? Do you believe that Friday and Saturday nights are the best times of your life? You're missing more than you think then. We've been brainwashed. We've been told to believe in the weekend more than we believe in our daily routine. But here's the scoop: you don't have to hate your mornings; you don't have to hate school; you don't have to hate your job. Who is to say that your Monday can't be as good as your Saturday?

Yes, you can live with passion every day of the week for every task in front of you. Sure, some of it may be more fun. But it's all part of your purpose in this life. Find your joy in every moment. You were born to learn and work and grow. So declare something new and believe that your best life exists **now**. Stop putting limits on your life and start expecting each day to be meaningful. God has more for you than just the "night show."

When Jesus saw him lying there and learned that he had been in this condition for a long time, he asked him, "Do you want to get well?"

JOHN 5:6

DAILY DECLARATION

I believe that life is meaningful every day and everything in my life is for a purpose.

don't hold back

_____

_____

_____

_____

_____

" your gifts are yours "

How good it is to be you! Have you ever thought that? God made you with some traits that he gave to no one else. The way you write. The way you smile. The way that you dance better than anyone in the room. The way your strong mind can deduce a problem in seconds. The way you love people beyond their faults. Whatever it is, you know you'll have that gift for life. It's yours. It has purpose in your hands; otherwise, God would have never allowed it to fall on you. Don't hide it; use it.

Show the world your gifts. Don't be afraid to dream big and go for it. You'll regret it if you don't leap. Match your gifts with passion, and you'll go far. So next time you scroll on Instagram and see what someone else is good at, remember what **you** hold. It's something they don't. Your authenticity is your power. Please don't let it go to waste.

GOD MADE YOU THIS WAY.
YOU DON'T NEED WHAT OTHERS HAVE.
KILLING COMPARISON STARTS WITH THANKFULNESS FOR WHAT YOU HAVE.

Let the peace of Christ rule in your hearts, since as members of one body you were called to peace. And be thankful.

COLOSSIANS 3:15

DAILY DECLARATION

It's good to be me! I know God has tailor-made me as me. Today, I will thank him for who I am.

don't hold back

_____

_____

_____

_____

_____

"you're in training"

There's something hard but beautiful about training. You may not agree with what you're learning now, but you will need it later. You are being prepared for something. There's no telling what will happen next year, or even next week. What's important to know is that your perspective holds a lot of power. But it's nearly impossible to learn from a situation that you don't believe has purpose. So let me encourage you by saying: Believe in what you're going through right now. Not because you are so happy or think highly of your "training," but because something good will come from it.

In times of training, you can't allow negativity to win. Practice is part of life, right? So much of everyday situations won't make sense until the "game" actually starts. Believe that your practice is who you are and getting you ready for what's around the corner.

THIS IS HARD BUT BEAUTIFUL.
TRAINING HAS A GREATER PURPOSE.
THIS IS PRACTICE.

> Surely your goodness and love will follow me all the days of my life, and I will dwell in the house of the LORD forever.
>
> **PSALM 23:6**

DAILY DECLARATION

I know God is working on this mosaic of mine. I will not let negativity draw me away from my training.

don't hold back

_____

_____

_____

_____

_____

"these are your voices"

Can you count how many voices are speaking into your life right now? If you can, you're probably better off than most. Voices hold power and often direct us toward our next destination. Do you **know** all the voices you're letting in? It's important that you keep tabs on each and every one—because before you know it, you could be letting something or someone direct you that you never asked for.

Look at your close friends. How powerful are their voices to you, and do they speak encouragement or death? Check what you listen to. What plays through your headphones? What do you watch? Yes, I'm getting personal because this matters. Every voice plays a part, and the ones that get more airtime will hold more power over your future. Some voices you may need to turn off; others, you may need to press pause. Turn up the volume on the voices you believe in. Let those be the ones you hear loud and clear.

VOICES HOLD A LOT OF POWER.
EVERY VOICE PLAYS A PART.
EACH VOICE EITHER SPEAKS LIFE OR DEATH.

Blessed are those who find wisdom, those who gain understanding, for she is more profitable than silver and yields better returns than gold.

PROVERBS 3:13–14

DAILY DECLARATION

God, let the voices in my life lead me to your best and lead by faith.

don't hold back

_____

_____

_____

_____

_____

"an important conversation"

Do you mean what you say? Better yet, do you mean what you pray? Any conversation can become weighty and complicated in our eyes. But prayer is a funny thing. Prayer is a conversation, only it isn't with the guy next to you, it's with your Creator.

Many people use it when the tough times hit and they feel like they need to make the call. But what about in the day-to-day? Or when others are watching? Or when it feels awkward? Prayer has power—and not just in private. Prayer that happens publicly is a special thing. I'm not talking about saying a few religious words to show off; I'm talking about boldly proclaiming your needs, your love, and your care. Don't be afraid of praying in public. It's a chance to show what you believe and be proud of who you do it for. Your prayer may make all the difference for someone around you.

YOU JUST HAVE TO START TALKING.
THERE'S POWER IN THIS.
PRAYER SPEAKS BOLDLY ABOUT YOUR FAITH.

"If you believe, you will receive whatever you ask for in prayer."

MATTHEW 21:22

DAILY DECLARATION

My prayers are powerful, and God is listening. I will be bold in what I say.

don't hold back

_____
_____
_____
_____
_____

"the friends you need"

It's easy to ride with people who talk the talk, but how about walk the walk? You need the ones who don't just call you to go out, but also who call to check in: "How's your family? How's your soul? How is everything actually going?" You need the truth speakers in your corner. You need friends who will call you out in order to make you a better person. You will need those types of friends for the rest of your life.

A great friend sticks closer than a "brother." This means they won't shy away when opposition comes. It means they will stick by you no matter the circumstances. Look around. Do you have that? Are those closest to you dreaming with you for the long haul? Or are you surrounded by a bunch of people who want nothing more than a shallow relationship? Your friendships will carry you further than you could ever imagine. The cards are in your hand; maybe you need to make some changes.

MAKE IT LONG TERM.
YOU NEED REAL RELATIONSHIPS.
FRIENDSHIPS WILL CARRY YOU OR CRIPPLE YOU.

Do not be misled: "Bad company corrupts good character."

1 CORINTHIANS 15:33

DAILY DECLARATION

God, give me the people I need on this journey and help me step away from those I don't.

don't hold back

_____

_____

_____

_____

_____

"have that conversation"

Have you ever really wanted to have an important conversation but you didn't know how to approach it? I feel ya. I've been there too. But someone in your life is begging for you to speak—and waiting for you to listen. A needed conversation is waiting for you to start it. Don't let fear of awkwardness, saying the wrong thing, or starting a fire get in the way. It's time you step up to have that heart-to-heart you were thinking about the other night. Chances are, you've wanted this conversation for weeks, and it's ruined your day and your sleep because it's all you can think or talk about. Today is the day.

Call that person, or better yet, get lunch together. Use your words to build a bridge. Someone needs to hear this. Someone needs you to hear them. Stop putting it off. This conversation isn't meant to harm; it's meant to heal. Healing doesn't happen by holding it in. Come on. It's time to spark some growth for both of you.

HARD CONVERSATIONS CAN BRING HEALING.
LISTEN TO SOMEONE.
MAKE THE CALL.

And do not forget to do good and to share with others, for with such sacrifices God is pleased.

HEBREWS 13:16

DAILY DECLARATION

God, help me speak up when I need to and have those hard conversations. I will speak healing words and listen with love.

don't hold back

_____

_____

_____

_____

_____

"this one is for them ..."

The world is big and hurt is real. Can you imagine what it would feel like to have no one to talk to? What about the misfits? The people who never seem to get the front end of the conversation. The ones who don't get invited to the party. It's time to give different people a seat at your table.

There's someone in your life right now who feels as if they have no one to turn to. You could be the light they so desperately need. My advice: it's time to shove your ego aside and reach out to those who need you most. Be more inviting. Show more generosity. Pay closer attention. Through you, someone can get a glimpse of what it looks like to be loved. You know the person who's on your mind. Go after them.

DON'T FORGET ABOUT THE OUTSIDERS.
INVITE THOSE WHO ARE DIFFERENT FROM YOU.
KEEP AN OPEN MIND AND HEART, FULL OF LOVE.

Then Jesus said to his host, "When you give a luncheon or dinner, do not invite your friends, your brothers or sisters, your relatives, or your rich neighbors; if you do, they may invite you back and so you will be repaid. But when you give a banquet, invite the poor, the crippled, the lame, the blind, and you will be blessed."

LUKE 14:12–14

DAILY DECLARATION

I'm inviting someone new into my life today and giving them my ears. People need people.

don't hold back

_____

_____

_____

"the night you've always wanted"

I don't know what you're stressed about or what worries have gotten hold of you, but you need a night to kick back. When was the last night you felt free? It's time you push your worries to the side and enjoy much needed time off. Take a break from the normal routine. That routine will lock you down if you don't learn to step out of it occasionally. If you spend all of your hours cramming in what you think needs to be done, it's only a matter of time before you explode. Come on, there's more to life than always minding your p's and q's.

Learn to ignite joy back into your bones and let go when life allows it. Find the friends you love and a good place to go, then take off. It's healthy for your soul. Now go, have some fun.

ENJOY SOME TIME OFF.
FIND WHAT YOU NEED.
REIGNITE YOUR JOY.

"Take my yoke upon you and learn from me, for I am gentle and humble in heart, and you will find rest for your souls. For my yoke is easy and my burden is light."

MATTHEW 11:29–30

DAILY DECLARATION

I'm finding joy in rest today. It's time to relax a little bit and take some time for me.

don't hold back

_____

_____

_____

_____

_____

"watch me work"

God is working. You aren't losing the battle like you think. Sometimes it's going to take a different perspective to see the work that's taking place in your world. God didn't fail you months or years ago, and he isn't starting now. I'm demanding a new season of faith for you.

Even as he works, you are being tested. "How can you not believe what I'm doing now?" God is saying to you. You've seen him do too much to walk in doubt. Don't you know something bigger is going on here? Nothing happens randomly. It may be that you need to do something you've never done before to see it all differently though. God is on the move and wants you to join in. You may be blind to it today, but if you let him, God will work on your vision. You'll see where and how he's working. You were meant to be a part of it. His story is yours too. Watch.

HE'S DOING SOMETHING.
OPEN YOUR EYES TO A NEW PERSPECTIVE.
START SHOWING UP.

Do not merely listen to the word, and so deceive yourselves. Do what it says. Anyone who listens to the word but does not do what it says is like someone who looks at his face in a mirror and ... immediately forgets what he looks like.

JAMES 1:22–24

DAILY DECLARATION

Lord, help me see what you are doing. It's time to take a step in the right direction.

don't hold back

"one thing leads to another"

Maybe you don't know the exact thing you need, but in your gut, you feel that something is going to shift for you. You need change for your health. Your family needs a new place to live. You need new friends. But what about that moment when what you were hoping for coincidentally shifts to something you never dreamed of? There's something special about the unexpected.

You may be in a place right now where you are hoping for one thing but God is interested in giving you another. Keep your options open. Don't let your own close-mindedness determine your life. Life is often a surprise, so be ready for anything. Be expectant today. What you are hoping will happen may not happen at all, and what you think is impossible may be the very thing God delivers to you.

EXPECT THE UNEXPECTED.
KEEP HOPING WITH AN OPEN MIND.
GOD DELIVERS SURPRISES.

Let us run with perseverance
the race marked out for us,
fixing our eyes on Jesus, the
pioneer and perfecter of faith.
For the joy set before him he
endured the cross, scorning its
shame, and sat down at the
right hand of the throne of God.

HEBREWS 12:1–2

DAILY DECLARATION

**God, keep my heart open to
what you have. I'm trusting in
what you have on the way.**

don't hold back

_____
_____
_____
_____
_____

"champion mentality"

I t starts here. Chase that passion. Build that dream. Learn to step like a champion. It means fighting when your mind wants to turn off. It means waking up even when everyone else chooses to sleep. The battle is not raging around you; it's inside you. Voices of contemplation and failure and timidity will work to keep you from going on. But champions aren't built overnight, and those habits you've been praying for won't appear in a mere twenty-four hours. This is going to take trial and error. So get ready for the long nights.

When your mind and heart work together, then you can take the steps you've always imagined. Persevere when others quit. So when decisions arise, you will be ready. Do the work others aren't willing to do.

CHASE THAT PASSION.
BRING ON THE LONG NIGHTS.
LIVE READY AT ALL TIMES.

For the Spirit God gave us does not make us timid, but gives us power, love and self-discipline.

2 TIMOTHY 1:7

DAILY DECLARATION

God, give me the strength in my mind and my heart to persevere. I am ready for what's to come.

don't hold back

_____

_____

_____

_____

_____

"stop running from community"

You've complained and pointed fingers for so long now. It's not working out because you are choosing isolation. You can't dare to think you can accomplish this all on your own? That frustration you're feeling? It's not because of others; it's because you need others but your pride keeps getting in the way. Learn to be honest with yourself. What are you holding back? What can't you let go of? Stop pushing them away. Stop placing blame elsewhere. This life is bigger than you and your own strength.

Find your people. Learn to lean on people so that in your weakness, in your fear, they can lift you above what holds you down. When you depend on others, you aren't just trusting in what they can do, but you're also believing in what God can do through others. He isn't one to put you down on your worst day. When you are most vulnerable, that's when God can act greatly within you. Open yourself up; others want to know you.

STOP THINKING YOU CAN DO IT BY YOURSELF.
YOUR OWN STRENGTH ISN'T ENOUGH.
IT'S YOU WHO NEEDS HELP.

When anxiety was great within me, your consolation brought me joy.

PSALM 94:19

DAILY DECLARATION

I put down my pride today. God, help me trust the community that believes in me.

don't hold back

_____

_____

_____

_____

_____

"the fears that eat you"

What is really scaring you? Is it failure? Is it fake friends? That you think they won't like you? That you'll always be behind? Fear can crush you. Yet you haven't realized how much your fears are affecting your grind. They're keeping you from action. You're staying in bed longer. You're holding yourself back. Your ambition is diminishing. On top of that, your dreams are suddenly on the back burner.

Fear has been nibbling away at you for too long. You can't stay in this spot, allowing it to devour what God wants to do in you. Pray for a mindset that will conquer. Choose faith. Day after day you must make a choice. You will not let fear have dominion over your life. Trust your God who loves you. Faith is stronger than any fear and chases it out the door.

CHOOSE FAITH NOT FEAR.
FIND STRENGTH IN God.
DON'T RUN FROM WHAT SCARES YOU.

"Be strong, do not fear; your God will come, he will come with vengeance; with divine retribution he will come to save you."

ISAIAH 35:4

DAILY DECLARATION

I'm looking my fears straight in the eyes and choosing faith today. I've been trapped for too long now. Not anymore.

don't hold back

_____

_____

_____

_____

_____

"friends and future"

Check the four to five people closest to you ASAP. What they say to you, how they encourage you, how they hang out with you—or if they do none of that. It all matters. A direct correlation exists between your friends and your future. All friendships point you in a direction, but do you know what direction that is? Where they point you now may be hard to change later. This means that you have to invest in who matters. You can't afford to be led astray because you want to please people for popularity and good laughs. Make sure you know these "friends" of yours and the impact they have on your day-to-day. The Lord knows who's there for purpose and who's there for pleasure. Open your ears to what people are speaking into your life. Are you confident in who is walking with you?

YOUR FRIENDS AFFECT YOUR FUTURE.
START PAYING ATTENTION.
YOU NEED PEOPLE WHO POINT YOU IN A GOOD DIRECTION.

One who has unreliable friends soon comes to ruin, but there is a friend who sticks closer than a brother.

PROVERBS 18:24

DAILY DECLARATION

God, give me friends who will walk alongside me to a healthy future. Keep my eyes peeled for those who aren't really for me.

don't hold back

_____

_____

_____

_____

_____

"hope has a name"

Where is the real hope? The real security? The real satisfaction? It's here. Yes, it exists, but you've been looking in all the wrong places. You've searched the social crowd, the sports teams, any hobby you can think of, and even young love—but nothing seems to be adding up for a full heart. Sure, you get a little spark, but it doesn't last.

Hope has a name. And he goes by Jesus. No girlfriend, no boyfriend, no fling, no thrill, no accomplishment can replace the kind of security that he offers. He invites you to come as you are, confusion and all. You may have baggage and a hard heart, but his arms are still open. See, true hope stays no matter the conditions. Let this hope lead you.

STOP SEARCHING IN THE WRONG PLACES.
YOU NEED REAL SECURITY.
COME AS YOU ARE.

May the God of hope fill you with all joy and peace as you trust in him, so that you may overflow with hope by the power of the Holy Spirit.

ROMANS 15:13

DAILY DECLARATION

God, give me the hope I need and help me find everything I need in you today.

don't hold back

_____

_____

_____

_____

_____

"it's not for everyone"

Where God has told you to go isn't for everyone. You may feel called to do things unlike any other—and that's okay. We each have a unique journey. No two of us are called to be the same or do the same in the same way. But everyone seems to have their own ideas of what **you** should do, don't they? "You're supposed to go here." "Be friends with them." "Pray for this." "Walk away from that." It's not easy hearing so many voices. So when others don't understand, turn your head and keep going. Focus on what you know is true.

When criticism is through the roof, listen to the right voices. When eyebrows rise, stay on course. Don't let them put a damper on your fire. See, you've been called to this. This place. This city. This pursuit. God has crafted it for you since the beginning of time. Stay faithful and keep walking the path he set out for you.

THERE'S SOMETHING SPECIAL ABOUT YOUR JOURNEY.
PEOPLE MAY CRITICIZE YOU.
STAY ON COURSE.

There are different kinds of gifts, but the same Spirit distributes them. There are different kinds of service, but the same Lord.

1 CORINTHIANS 12:4-5

DAILY DECLARATION

God is taking me somewhere, and even if others question it, it's for my good and his glory.

don't hold back

_____

_____

_____

_____

_____

"notice me"

Have you ever wished that others would see you? Are you hoping to be noticed for once? I'm not talking about the Instagram you or the Fortnite you or the beautiful Pinterest board you, but the real you. You know—the one they see every day at school, in the hall, on the field, and at home. Maybe it's your own family who fails to see you. The world can seem like a lonely place. Yet you deserve to be seen because you were meant to be known. And God knows you, the real you. He sees you. Didn't you know? He created you for a purpose. You were no accident. I don't care what Mom or Dad said when they left; you were born for something.

So today I stand with you and notice who you are. Believe that even when others "forget" to see you for you, God approves of you. He loves you. So be confident in your skin because it's yours to rock. You are no longer fighting for approval from those who don't seem to care. You are living for God.

YOU WERE MEANT TO BE KNOWN.
GOD APPROVES OF YOU.
YOU ARE NOT AN ACCIDENT.

For we are God's handiwork,
created in Christ Jesus to
do good works, which God
prepared in advance for us
to do.

EPHESIANS 2:10

DAILY DECLARATION

**God sees me for who I am. I will
not waste my life fighting for
attention from those around me.**

don't hold back

_____
_____
_____
_____
_____

"from hurt to healing"

A day will come when your hurts promote you to something better. I don't mean that you always need pain to gain, but you do need pain to experience healing. I know that's where you've been—a place of pain. The death you felt, the loss, the confusion of where you're headed hurts so badly. Good news: healing is here. Hurt no longer has the higher ground because you are moving forward. You are leaving what happened behind.

Healing is being offered to you. God is saying, "Here, take this now." Reach out. Grab it. Let your heart fill with a sense of promise. Even though you haven't received all the answers you want, healing is making its way in you. Pain doesn't win, and it never will because you've got something greater in your blood: a God who always heals.

HEALING IS ON THE WAY.
YOU HAVE A FUTURE.
YOUR PAIN IS NOT PERMANENT.

I consider that our present sufferings are not worth comparing with the glory that will be revealed in us.

ROMANS 8:18

DAILY DECLARATION

I know this pain isn't forever. God will heal me, and in due time, I will see something greater.

don't hold back

_____

_____

_____

_____

_____

"worry, worry"

You've let worries take the wheel so you're spinning around and around. What will worry do for you, anyway? It only creates fear of situations that may or may not come to be. It ties you up in knots. See, you're overthinking it. When you allow those worries to grow, they crush the trust God calls you to have in him. Ya know? Trust the process. It's okay if you can't see it all. Sometimes that's the better way to live because then you have to choose trust.

What you're worried about is most likely a small piece of the puzzle. And if you let that feeling of uncertainty control you day after day, you'll never succeed in walking with peace. Ease your mind. Let go and welcome God to take over. Your story is still being written, and it's a good one.

\# KILL YOUR WORRIES.
\# TRUST God's PROCESS; IT BRINGS PEACE.
\# RENEW YOUR MIND DAY BY DAY.

Do not be anxious about anything, but in every situation, by prayer and petition, with thanksgiving, present your requests to God.

PHILIPPIANS 4:6

DAILY DECLARATION

Worry will not rule my mindset any longer. I will trust God's control and live in his peace.

don't hold back

_____

_____

_____

_____

_____

"stop speaking death"

I t's okay to critique your life, but when those words become the deathbed of your potential, that's an issue. Your own words are crushing you, and it's time you recognize the sharpness of your tongue. You hold a lot of power with your words. When you speak your own frustrations over your body, they leave a mark inside your mind and heart. When you speak highly of yourself, not to boast but to encourage, it builds you up.

You can't speak death to your own soul any longer. You are better than that. There's more to who you are. You are becoming someone. You are in a process. Sure, your hair may not be just the way you like it. You may not be as smart as the next guy. Maybe your "profile" doesn't add up to a teammate's, or you wish your parents were still together because life was easier then. But your life is not over. Take responsibility for what you say to yourself. Speak life—because your life matters.

DON'T DO THIS TO YOURSELF.
YOUR LIFE IS NOT OVER.
YOUR WORDS HOLD POWER.

The tongue of the wise adorns knowledge, but the mouth of the fool gushes folly.

PROVERBS 15:2

DAILY DECLARATION

I will speak life over myself today, because I'm worth something. There's more to my story than what I see at the moment.

don't hold back

_____

_____

_____

_____

_____

"there's a place for you"

God has seen you all along, whether you believe in him or not. Just because you haven't seen something special in yourself doesn't mean it doesn't exist. You've spent countless hours believing the lie that the person next to you—the one with the better pictures, the person with more followers—has a place and you don't. Why are you focused on that person? That lie has knocked out every ounce of confidence in you. The truth? You have talent, and there is a place for you. But it's a place that you will have to take with courage. Don't miss out on what is waiting for you. God set it up for you long ago. Be confident that you have a place with your name all over it. Don't focus on what you think may happen; focus on where he has put you and why he chose you. When you see that with faith, your confidence will soar.

GOD HASN'T FORGOTTEN YOU.
DON'T BELIEVE THE LIES.
BE CONFIDENT IN WHAT YOU'VE GOT.

And if I go and prepare a place for you, I will come back and take you to be with me that you also may be where I am.

JOHN 14:3

DAILY DECLARATION

I've not been left behind. I was made for something. I have confidence today.

don't hold back

_____

_____

_____

_____

_____

"when the depression traps you"

I don't want to see your thoughts hold you hostage anymore. This sickness, this attack (yes, that's what it is) that we call depression will not break you down. Life doesn't stop here. It's time to let community in. It's time to have conversations. And no, a Netflix binge or iPhone scrolling will not do the trick.

We are all broken people who need people. Don't allow yourself to sit here alone. When the first person reaches out to you, take their hand. And if you already let them pass you by, go back. Depression does not have to win. People are on your team. You are loved; you have purpose; you're meant for life outside of this mental prison. We will not allow this to get the last word over your story. I believe in you. Accept the help you need.

TAKE THE HAND.
LET COMMUNITY IN.
OTHERS BELIEVE IN YOU.

Many are saying of me, "God will not deliver him." But you, LORD, are a shield around me, my glory, the One who lifts my head high.

PSALM 3:2–3

DAILY DECLARATION

Lord, I'm declaring a new hope over my life. Bring people who will lift me up. Show me that I'm not alone in this fight.

don't hold back

_____

_____

_____

_____

_____

"you have a voice"

Sometimes your silence is needed, but at other times, you need to be vocal. Whether you realize it or not, you have a voice. And not just any voice, but **your** voice. Your ideas mean something, and your "say" is important.

God gave you a voice that can impact your community, your social media, your world. If sitting around silent is what you've been doing for months now, that voice is going to waste. You don't have to be loud or arrogant or power hungry, but you do need to speak up. The longer you fail to use what God gave you, the more you'll see change fail to happen. Use that voice. Being vocal doesn't mean being ugly, but it gives you an opportunity to spark something. What will you spark?

- # IT'S TIME TO SPEAK UP.
- # YOUR WORDS CARRY POWER, AND THEY DON'T HAVE TO BE LOUD.
- # YOUR VOICE MATTERS.

For I am not ashamed of the gospel, because it is the power of God that brings salvation to everyone who believes: first to the Jew, then to the Gentile.

ROMANS 1:16

DAILY DECLARATION

I've got something to say. I can't be silent any longer.

don't hold back

_____

_____

_____

_____

_____

"more circles"

We've grown up in a society that constantly puts things in order. We make an assigned row for every person or idea. We like categories. You've probably seen it in your school or your job. We need order, but sometimes it gets in the way of including others and having conversations. We don't need more rows or alignment. We need bigger hearts. We need to create circles. Circles offer not only comfort, but circles give birth to conversations.

Do you realize what you could change if you created a circle rather than a row? Rows put others in a place, and circles offer space to talk. And in conversation, that's where we learn and grow. So why not create a life of "circles?" Open up to new conversations, and welcome people in even when it messes with the perfect "order." You know we need each other. Keep building each other up and friendships will last. Relationships will flourish. This is how we build the lives we've imagined.

HAVE A HEART.
CREATE CONVERSATIONS.
CIRCLES OFFER SPACE.

Carry each other's burdens,
and in this way you will fulfill
the law of Christ.

GALATIANS 6:2

DAILY DECLARATION

God, give me confidence to be
vulnerable and create circles for
much needed conversations.

don't hold back

_____

_____

_____

_____

_____

"friends aren't forever"

It's hard to swallow this one: People don't always stay. You may have heard this a million times. You may have even wished against it, but it'll happen to you. Some of your best friends may move on. Some of your family may leave—or already have. When a season suddenly changes, some people change too. You must know that things just aren't forever. I don't know if this is a wake-up call, but I'd rather you hear it now than be hurt by it later.

So now what? That's what you're probably wondering. It's time we stop placing hope in people who will change, move, and even let us down. We must hope in what will last. The question is, what are you believing in for your forever? Do you have faith? Are you living by it? Or is it only a crutch when life gets tough? Hope in what's real. Hope in who your God is.

TRUTH MAY HURT.
PEOPLE MAY LET YOU DOWN.
FIND HOPE IN WHAT LASTS.

We have this hope as an anchor for the soul, firm and secure. It enters the inner sanctuary behind the curtain.

HEBREWS 6:19

DAILY DECLARATION

My hope is bigger than myself and the people in it. This hope anchors my soul.

don't hold back

_____

_____

_____

_____

_____

"learning with the burn"

I f you're honest, are you hanging around with people and/or doing things that have huge potential to burn you? Decisions are tough when you enjoy someone or something so much. But fire is fire and it's dangerous to play with. When you do, you put yourself in a position to fall over and over again. Maybe you've felt the pain once or twice and made a change. You knew a person was toxic, so you walked away. Or you made a move before a risky situation got too close. But nobody is perfect, and you won't always have clear eyes. So it's important that you learn with the burn.

When you feel the fire of something that's not right in your life, step back and get real. If you fail to recognize the lesson, then you risk a lot of senseless pain. Because if you play around with fire too long, you won't just get burned, but you'll burn up your future.

\# **YOU'LL SUCCEED BY LEARNING FROM THE BURN.**
\# **STEP BACK AND LET YOUR VISION CLEAR.**
\# **STOP PLAYING WITH FIRE.**

I will instruct you and teach
you in the way you should
go; I will counsel you with my
loving eye on you.

PSALM 32:8

DAILY DECLARATION

**God, I'm going to learn as I go.
Help me on the way.**

don't hold back

_____

_____

_____

_____

_____

"when frustration sets in"

C an you just be honest? Life isn't the best for you right now. It is what it is, and a smile may be hard to come by. You may not be feeling the love you think you should. Reality is that we all get tired of life. You may want others to see what you are doing and think "perfection" or "they're never worried," but it's hard to keep up with that. And life doesn't always cooperate, does it?

Here's the deal: sometimes you have to make do with what you've been given, frustrations and all. When frustration sets in, honestly speak about what you are going through, where you are, and what's hurting. You are a work in progress, but aren't we all? So here's to being open and real. Don't be afraid to share what's going on. We all have a season to share.

LEARN TO MAKE DO WITH WHAT IS.
YOU AREN'T CALLED TO BE PERFECT.
SHARE OPENLY AND HONESTLY.

Be very careful, then, how you live—not as unwise but as wise, making the most of every opportunity, because the days are evil.

EPHESIANS 5:15–16

DAILY DECLARATION

I'm going to make the most out of nothing because God has given me this day.

don't hold back

_____

_____

_____

_____

_____

"gimme the details"

Sometimes you feel like you have to have every answer in order to succeed or go to the next level. That's no way to live. It's not realistic. Striving for that kind of control is distracting and runs us away from the greater mission. You don't need the perfect grades, perfect outfit, and perfect social media feed to do what you were made to do. You don't even need to know where the next road leads—whether to college or that dream job. Yes, seek the details, but don't cling to them. Breathe and take life one day at a time, one task at a time.

Here's what you can remember: the world is not on **your** shoulders. God is not counting on **you** every second of the day. His higher power is at work. Life will be okay. So look forward to what today will bring. It's the only day you've got.

GO ONE STEP AT A TIME.
THE WORLD ISN'T ON YOUR SHOULDERS.
LEARN TO BREATHE.

Cast all your anxiety on him because he cares for you.

1 PETER 5:7

DAILY DECLARATION

God is covering the details. I don't carry all the weight, and I don't need all the answers.

don't hold back

_____

_____

_____

_____

_____

don't hold back